# Dogku:

dog haiku poems

Other books by the same authors:

Catku
Horseku
Petku
RESKU

# Dogku:

## dog haiku poems

by

Ginny Tata-Phillips and Diane Grindol

**second edition**

Second Edition published 2010
Printed by CreateSpace.com in
the United States of America

First Edition published 2008
Printed by CafePress.com in
the United States of America

\

Unless otherwise noted, cover photos
and photos throughout
this book are by Diane Grindol

# Contents

# Thanks!

Thank you, Gwen Roberts:
my daughter, my friend, and now,
my best editor!
*gtp*

Efficient and true,
a sharp eye and a sharp wit.
Ginny's editing.
*-dg*

# Introduction

These are haiku poems, a form of Japanese poetry with strict rules.

| | |
|---|---|
| **First line** | **5 syllables** |
| **Second line** | **7 syllables** |
| **Third line** | **5 syllables** |

That's it. A poem in three lines. Traditionally they are about nature. Our poems don't have the traditional theme, only the haiku structure.

To write our poems, both of us were inspired by our real lives living with and caring for dogs. Rather than write out our full names, we have initialed each poem.

Ginny Tata-Phillips (gtp) and Diane Grindol (-dg)

By writing Haiku
Ginny Tata-Phillips keeps
hold of sanity
*gtp*

Diane Grindol writes
pet sits and does photography
Extraordinary!
*gtp*

# Authors

**Ginny Tata-Phillips**
Although relatively new to haiku, Ginny has been writing since the days of "How I Spent My Summer Vacation." She advanced through school essays to term papers, letters to the editor, newsletter and magazine articles. She has been a dog lover for 50 years; a dog owner for 40 and involved in dog-related businesses for 20. Ginny and her husband ran a successful doggy daycare center and boarding facility in California. She now lives in Central Florida with 5 rescued dogs and assorted birds, fish, reptiles and amphibians. She currently composes while pet sitting and dog walking (5-7-5, 5-7-5) and rushes home to write down her real-life-inspired dogku.

Ginny
Tata-Phillips (left)

Diane Grindol
(right)

**Diane Grindol**
Diane received her first dog at age 8 and started pet sitting at age 10. In fifth grade she was introduced to haiku poetry, and loved it. She has become inspired to revisit its simple, challenging format again as an adult. Diane is currently a full time pet sitter. She has owned dogs, including a rescued Briard she showed in obedience. She does freelance photography of pets and their people. Diane lives in Pacific Grove, California, with cockatiels, a blue-headed pionus parrot and a guinea pig.

It's the count and not
the cadence that make haiku
five – seven – five. End.

-dg

# A Dog's Life

We created dogs
for sport and hunt and leisure;
they all give back love.

*-dg*

Life is good until
evil nail clippers appear.
Quick!  Under the bed!

*gtp*

Life is great until
bath preparation begins.
Quick!  Behind the chair!

*gtp*

Life is fine until
ear cleaning supplies show up.
Quick!  Run away fast!

*gtp*

Lick granuloma.
Obsessive-compulsive act
of a lonely dog.

Pup frenzy precedes
complete meltdown surrender
to profound limp sleep.

-dg

The best thing about
a fire hydrant is that it's
never occupied.

Best pals frolic, play;
posture, and chase through the surf
on a bright beach day.

-dg

Thirst finally slaked,
the bewhiskered dog leaves a
trail of drips behind.

-dg

Self-assured puppy
follows its new master home.
At night, brief whimpers.
-dg

Strewn across the bed
in repose dogs look harmless;
a noise, they're all bark.

Sit! Stay! Down! Place! Heel!
Commands? Requests asked of an
obedient dog.

*gfp*

Bloodhounds seem to be basset hounds that just could not stop growing taller.

*gtp*

Basset hounds are just
ears, noses and long bodies
housing angel's souls.

*glp*

Distemper, parvo, rabies; all avoidable when we vaccinate.

*gtp*

Duties are many:
guard, defend, locate, obey
'til well-earned sleep comes.

*-dg*

Some itchy places
a dog can't reach require a
good hard twisting roll.
-dg

Basket full of toys,
why can't the puppy resist
lure of underwear?

*gtp*

Loyal and true friend.
Forever loved. Truly missed.
Ashes on mantle.

Dogs and humans drool
over the smell of home-made
dog cookies baking.
*-dg*

The fleet hound has two
speeds: one fast as the wind, one
saving energy.

-dg

At six bells the dogs
roar awake, inhale kibble,
then go back to sleep.

*-dg*

Rudolph's antlers are askew and his smile is weak. He's adorable!

My vocal Basset
points nose to ceiling and howls.
No rhyme or reason.

*glp*

Since the neutering,
he licks himself in tribute
to what used to be.

*glp*

A man said to me,
"She's the dog a boy would draw;
his own perfect dog."

The wiry-haired dog
was ever after made of
crayon strokes, scribbles.

*-dg*

Jingle-jangle of
tags on the dish means dinner
is being consumed.

-dg

A mound of kibble
is devoured by a hungry
dog in two minutes.
-dg

Cat feet bring the fog.
Dog feet pound the snow; wild howls
stir the restless winds.

*-dg*

Tentative dog steps
walk over me in feigned sleep;
to wake is to play.

Hound trounced small dog, who
squealed and defiantly peed
on his way out gate.
-dg

While a child learns and adults toil, the dog waits for happy home-coming.

*-dg*

# Those Who Serve

Search and Rescue Dogs:
the most talented noses
find those who are lost.

*glp*

Dogs earn badges when
they serve and protect just like
humans.  Police Dogs.
*gtp*

Detecting seizures
sniffing out cancers, bombs, drugs.
Miracle noses.

glp

Guide Dogs. Kind. Patient.
If I lead will you follow?
Let me be your eyes.

*glp*

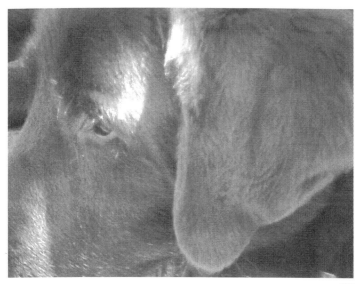

# Canine Perspective

*Photo by Amber Thompson*

Why do you scoop my poop so carefully yet freak if I consume it?

*gfp*

"I am getting fixed?
Did not know I was broken,"
he cried to the vet.

*glp*

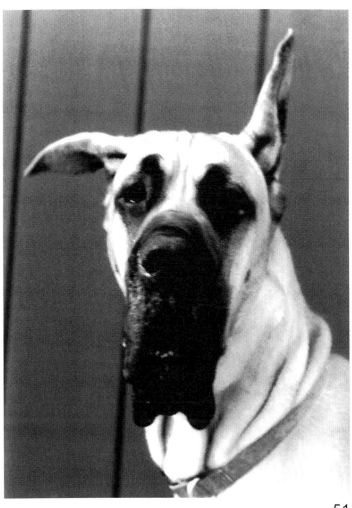

BARK BARK BARK BARK BARK.
Short man syndrome strikes again.
BARK BARK BARK BARK BARK.
*gtp*

Mom and Dad feel in
the mood.  At the foot of the
bed I make stinkies.

*gfp*

Only my nose fits
this hole in my garden gate.
It's a peer-less gate.

*-dg*

I dig because I
know there is something better
underneath that dirt.

*gtp*

I am a proper
British gentleman called the
English Setter dog!

*gtp*

I may seem at rest
but ears are always cocked for
treat jar opening!

*gtp*

You are what you eat.
I'm supper crumbs and garbage,
dog treats and tissues.

*-dg*

How do I love thee?
By rolling in something dead,
rotten or smelly.

*gtp*

We are wolves, the true descendents of packs of wild dogs come to the fire.

*-dg*

CAR RIDE! Ears flying --
head hanging, window open.
Oh joy!  I smell beach!

CAR RIDE! Ears flying --
head hanging, window open.
Oh no!  I smell vet!

I've got my sea legs;
this Keeshound  knows how  to keep
the captain's boat safe
*-dg*

Bright and perky I
may be. Always ready to
walk or play with you.

*glp*

We were left alone
but we aren't alone; you are
coming and we wait.

*-dg*

I lied; it's too hard.
Interminable waiting.
Toilet paper fun.

*-dg*

Seemingly asleep,
nose quivering; I am on
guard, always alert.

I may be old but
I still love the seashore; waves
kids, birds; lots of fun!

*gtp*

My name is Bond, James Bond. I am a Scottish dog of great distinction!

*g/p*

Sugar Rae; lover
not a fighter despite my
famous boxing name!

*glp*

By sheer force of will
I know I can make this ball
throw itself for me.

-dg

Obedience is
just one of my talents, though
I am a Dachshund!

*gtp*

Your every wish is
my command. I live to love
and you are the ONE!

*glp*

There's always a spot
on a dog's belly where the
rear foot engages.

-dg

I'm the top dog by
a growl, eat first, get treats first;
top dog among dogs.
*-dg*

From my spot in the sun, I contemplate life, which is all good to me.

*gtp*

*Photo by Evelyn Dufner*

With longer legs I
bet I could drive this car, but
why would I want to?

*glp*

*Photo by Evelyn Dufner*

There's the garage door.
Check list: get off the couch now.
Sit, adoring gaze.

In the morning, first
the dog undoes its muscles
in a long slow stretch.

*-dg*

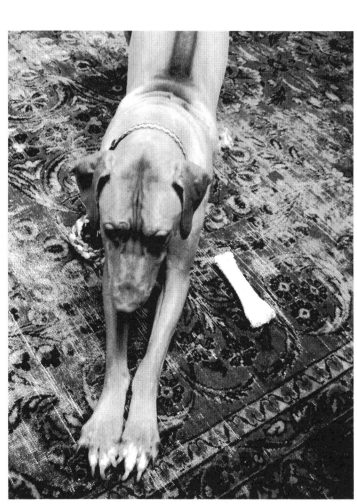

# Human Perspective

A three pound dog fits
under my chin overnight,
barks at intruders.

I try to be the
Dog Whisperer but am more
like the Dog Yeller.

*gtp*

Puppy terrorist;
a few good years, then decline.
Her life is too short.

Once this beauty show
ends we will  be *really* out
standing in our field.

-dg

It is good to have
an example of boundless
joy and love of life!

The influence of
a dog on life is out of
proportion to size.
-dg

I can't imagine
how changed my life would be if
I had passed you by.
*-dg*

My Greyhound is so
very  relaxed in the ring.
Long down? No problem.
*-dg*

Fawn, tawny, golden,
tan, red, liver or chocolate.
It's all brown to me.

Slower step, grey face
cloudy eyes.  My good old dog -
your heart ever young.

*gtp*

Hot breath and panting;
I open my eyes to a
dog who wants *out*... now.
-dg

My Dalmation is
a living Rorschach ink blot.
We test visitors.

*-dg*

"Out, out damn spot" is
rarely heard in a house with
regal Dalmations!

*gtp*

Beauty is inside
my short-nosed, wrinkled, snoring
loving, sweet Pug dog.
*-dg*

All she asks of life
is laps, reassurance and
occasional treats
*-dg*

While preparing lunch
I sense that I am watched by
patient, hopeful eyes.

-dg

A weekend morning
is the same to the dogs as
weekdays. Up at six!

*-dg*

Cockapoos used to
be the only mixed up dogs,
without high price tags.

*gtp*

A trick of nature
put a male dog in poodle
curls; delicate bones.

*-dg*

No one dares enter
our yard, because they know not
our hound's kind, sweet heart.

-dg

With proper Schnauzer
alacrity we march down
the street and back home.

My red dog is such
a red fox. A small husky?
We keep them guessing.
-dg

I got a new shirt.
"Professional Dog Walker -
Frequent Stops" it says.
*-dg*

The good dogs are old,
worn-in, grizzled. Love in eyes
covered by blue film.

-dg

She runs away and
she pees on the bathroom rug:
cute is forgiven!

*-dg and gtp*

My dog and I are
still a work in progress. We
watch from the sidelines.
*-dg*

Plush dog toy is the
only well-behaved canine
here. Listens to me!

*-dg*

He's noble, he's fleet.
Deerhounds are statuesque dogs
of short acquaintence.

It's a small thing to
fetch the paper and return,
but we are both proud.

Unwanted puppies --
sad eyes, small shelter cages.
Please spay or neuter!

*gtp*

**We're the proud authors of these haiku/photo books:**

Dogku
Catku
Horseku
Petku
RESKU (rescued dogs)

We welcome your photos and stories about your beloved pets, to include in future books. Pets only please, we won't include photos that include people in the picture.

**Contact the authors:**

Diane Grindol
PO Box 51247
Pacific Grove CA 93950

dgrindol@yahoo.com

Ginny Tata-Phillips
10126 Bayard Ct.
Orlando FL 32836

my4hounds@hotmail.com

**You've read many tales
of tails; loyalty and love,
and this is the end.**
*-dg*

Made in the USA
Middletown, DE
06 September 2018